DESCARTES AMONG THE SCHOLASTICS

The Aquinas Lecture, 1991

DESCARTES AMONG THE SCHOLASTICS

Under the auspices of the
Wisconsin-Alpha Chapter of Phi Sigma Tau

by

MARJORIE GRENE

Marquette University Press
Milwaukee
1991

Library of Congress Catalogue Number: 90-64234.

Copyright 1991

Marquette University Press

ISBN 0-87462-158-5.

Prefatory

The Wisconsin-Alpha Chapter of Phi Sigma Tau, the National Honor Society for Philosophy at Marquette University, each year invites a scholar to deliver a lecture in honor of St. Thomas Aquinas.

The 1991 Aquinas Lecture, *Descartes Among the Scholastics*, was delivered in the Tony and Lucille Weasler Auditorium on Sunday, February 24, 1991, by Marjorie G. Grene, Professor Emeritus of Philosophy, University of California, Davis, and Honorary Distinguished Professor, Virginia Polytechnic Institute and State University.

Professor Grene was born in Milwaukee and received her B.A. from Wellesley College. She received her M.A. and Ph.D. from Radcliffe College, Harvard University. After beginning her teaching career at Monticello College, Marjorie Grene went on to teach at the University of Chicago, Northwestern University, the University of Manchester, the University of Leeds, and Queen's University, Belfast. She has been Visiting Professor at the University of Texas, Austin, Boston University, the University of Göttingen, Tulane University, Temple University, Rutgers University, the University of California, Berkeley, Yale University, the University of Waterloo, Boston University, Vassar College, Rochester

Institute of Technology, Carleton College, the State University of New York at Binghamton, and Senior Research Fellow of Linacre College, Oxford. She was professor at the University of California, Davis, from 1965 to 1978.

Professor Grene was Virginia Gildersleeve Visiting Professor at Barnard College, 1987. She received an honorary doctorate from Tulane in 1980. She has served as President of the Pacific Division of the American Philosophical Association in 1971-1972 and of the Metaphysical Society of America in 1975-1976. She is a fellow of the American Academy of Arts and Sciences since 1976 and of the American Association for the Advancement of Science since 1977.

Among her books are: *Dreadful Freedom: A Critique of Existentialism* (1948; reissued, 1959 and 1984), *Heidegger* (1957), *A Portrait of Aristotle* (1963; reissued, 1967 and 1979), *The Knower and the Known* (1966, 1974, 1983), *Approaches to a Philosophical Biology* (1969), *Sartre* (1973; reprinted, 1983), *The Understanding of Nature: Essays in Philosophy of Biology* (1974), *Philosophy In and Out of Europe* (1976, reprinted 1987), and *Descartes* (1985). She has also edited eight books and published over eighty articles.

To Professor Grene's distinguished list of publications, Phi Sigma Tau is pleased to add: *Descartes Among the Scholastics*.

Acknowledgements

The part of this lecture that deals with substantial forms was given in a somewhat different form, and different language, as a lecture at the University of Bern and published in *Dialectica* under the title "Die Einheit des Menschen: Descartes unter den Scholastikern." I am grateful to the Editor of *Dialectica* for his kind permission to use the material here.

I must also acknowledge my indebtedness to Roger Ariew for many conversations on the subject matter of this lecture and for supplying material I might not otherwise have noticed. I have learned a great deal even from my disagreements with him. Father Roland Teske has corrected some of my historical errors, and I would like to thank him for his help.

Needless to say, I am most of all grateful to Marquette University for giving me the occasion to pursue a little further the all but inexhaustible topic of the scholastic context of Cartesian philosophy.

M.G.

DESCARTES AMONG THE SCHOLASTICS

*On ne peut comprendre le cartésianisme sans
le confronter continuellement avec cette
scolastique qu'il dédaigne, mais au sein du
laquelle il s'installe et dont, puisqu'il
l'assimile, on peut bien dire qu'il se
nourrit.* – E. Gilson, "Anthropologie Tho-
miste et Anthropologie Cartésienne," in
**Etudes sur le Rôle de la Pensée Médiévale
dans la Formation du Système Cartésien**,
Paris: Vrin, 1975 (lst ed., 1930), pp. 245-
255, p. 255.

The above epigram may serve as a text for
my lecture. Although its Gallic rhetoric cannot
easily be Englished, its theme is clear. We cannot
understand the Cartesian philosophy unless we
constantly confront it with the scholasticism it dis-
dains – so far, so good. But at the same time,
Gilson argues, Cartesian thought makes its home
within scholasticism, assimilates it and so is nourished by it. Throughout his long and fruitful
career, that was the thesis of Gilson's Cartesian
scholarship, from his dissertation on freedom in

Descartes and theology (Gilson, 1913b) and the invaluable Cartesio-scholastic index (Gilson, 1913a), through the magisterial edition of the *Discourse* (Gilson, 1926) to the collected essays on the role of medieval thought in the formation of the Cartesian system (Gilson, 1930), from which our text is drawn. Since apart from his Cartesian scholarship, Gilson was an eminent Thomist philosopher, who, incidentally, gave the Aquinas lecture at Marquette forty-four years ago, in 1947 (Gilson, 1947), and again in 1951 (Gilson, 1951), and since, from the time I first taught the *Meditations*, over fifty years ago, my reading, and teaching, of that seminal text have been formed by Gilson's interpretation, it seems appropriate on this occasion to pay tribute to his work.

What I want to do is very simple. I want to show you, chiefly through adducing some examples, how Gilson's thesis of Descartes's debt to scholasticism has been vindicated by recent scholarship. At the same time, Gilson's general theme has also been rendered subtler and more complex by the work of a great many scholars, not only French historians of philosophy directly in the Gilson tradition, but also, happily, a number of younger compatriots of ours who are giving, in my view at least, more life and interest to the history of modern philosophy than it has had for many decades. To avoid boring you with too many names and titles, I am appending to this lecture a bibliographical note and reference list that will, I hope, give you some idea where to look for some of this fascinating work, both confirmatory and elaborative. I will of course refer to some of it in the course of my discussion, particularly the first part of the lecture, in which I will suggest very sketchily both the reaffirmation of Gilson's position and some of the refinements or modifications of it suggested by recent scholarship, none of it my own. Then I want to consider in more detail one, thoroughly Gilsonian, example, to which I have myself given some thought – thought to which I was stimulated, in fact, by the work of one of those younger scholars to whom I shall refer in due course. This is the case of the concept of substantial form, a concept Descartes needed to eliminate in order to construct his new physics, but which he retained (or revived?) in one special context in the metaphysic on which that physics had eventually to be based.

****

Although the conception of Descartes as the founder of modern philosophy is a true truism, it has done a lot of harm, particularly at the hands of those who are so fascinated by the hyperbolic scepticism of the first Meditation that they never see beyond it. They never ask *why* Descartes wanted to lead the mind away from the senses, and to what, but move off to their present-day concerns with their version of scepticism or their worries about mind and brain, or what you will. The chief change in emphasis in Cartesian scholarship that I want to call your attention to here consists in the stress on Descartes, not in patches and as *our* contemporary, but in his whole *oeuvre* and as a thinker of his time. Nor, be it said, am I thinking of history practiced in a cheap sociological fashion, where social and political events are seen as the sole causes of ideas and philosophical issues are reduced to empty gestures, but of a subtler and more difficult, but more fruitful mode of conceptual history, in which one takes into account the intellectual climate of the time, tries to read at least some of the authors our author read or might have read, and so attempts to see the problems he faced as he may have seen them.

Now admittedly, to look hard at so-called Cartesian scepticism is not as such necessarily to approach its purveyor ahistorically. Sceptical literature was indeed well-established and widely read and noticed in Descartes's time, and he knew it well; but it was a literature he was using for a purpose, and not one that was the be-all and end-all of his serious readers' interest either. He even apologized for rehashing that old stuff (AT VII, 130). In short, I would argue, as Gilson did, that

Descartes's aim in the **Meditations** and the **Principles** was attuned to the scholastic reader and *a fortiori*, I would add, not much to the fashionable adherents of scepticism.

Wolfson called Spinoza "the last of the mediaevals" (Wolfson, 1934, p. vii). That is a little unfair to Spinoza, and it would be even more unfair to Descartes to call him that, but he was clearly trained in one, perhaps especially sophisticated, version of scholastic philosophy, and in the **Meditations** he was clearly addressing readers steeped in the same thought style. As Gilson put it so eloquently in his edition of the **Discourse**, where Montaigne and other sceptics wanted to doubt in order to verify our ignorance, Descartes practiced the technique of doubt in order to verify truth: his critique tended, Gilson wrote, *à vérifier la vérité* (Gilson, 1926, p. 269). And although of course Descartes did *say* that for this purpose he needed to overthrow all his former opinions, all he *really* wanted to overthrow was just so much of what his teachers had taught him as would enable him to construct a metaphysical foundation for the new mathematical physics, an emerging discipline in which, when he made his first essay into metaphysics, in 1629-30, he had already developed an interest. True, those changes would prove fateful, indeed, to the tradition that had nourished him, but I doubt if

Descartes had any conception how fateful they would be. More of that later. Meantime I would just make two points in defence of Descartes's announced conception of his enterprise.

First, what he is overturning in the *Meditations* is "all his former opinions," but opinions are easily overthrown, since their contradictory is always conceivable, and even defensible by somebody or other. In contrast, the scholastic maxims he evokes, for example, in the proofs of God in Meditation III, are known to him by natural light – and that is not opinion, but truth!

Secondly, sometimes, admittedly, he uses language of a traditional, Aristotelian cast in a way that appears chiefly rhetorical: the several, rather inconsistent, uses he makes of the notion of "material falsity," for example, seem to me to indicate a rather light-hearted use of concepts familiar to his readers, but scarcely central to his own arguments or beliefs. I don't for a moment believe Descartes held a solemnly worked out theory of material falsity: form-matter thinking is really foreign to his aims and methods. Yet if, as Dan Garber has argued, the *Meditations* constitute a dialogue with his contemporaries (Garber, 1986), or, as Ed Curley puts it, a dialectical progression in which he hoped to carry his scholastic readers with him (Curley, 1986), that was a reasonable way to talk: one uses one's reader's language when one can. Descartes is neither a liar nor a hypocrite, but a superb philosophical rhetorician, using the concepts and vocabulary available to him, to effect, as he hopes, a radical change in our approach to the knowledge of nature.

I cannot say that, even in passing, however, without recalling the incompatibility of rhetoric and philosophy as Plato saw it in the *Gorgias*. As a 20th century American, bombarded by our political as well as our commercial advertising, I am inclined to agree that rhetoric as such is fraudulent. Still, to worry about that here would take me too far afield. Let us suppose for now that there can be, and is, acceptable philosophical rhetoric – indeed, Plato himself transcendently exemplifies it. And so, in his less dramatizing way, does Descartes. Again, to return to the point I was distracted from by a twinge of Platonic conscience, Descartes is using the conceptual apparatus of his contemporaries in order to bring about a radical change, not in *all* their concepts, but in the method as well as the content of their physics.

Such a change, Descartes has found, has to be mediated by a change in the approach to knowledge itself and to the mind of the knower; it even produces, as Gilson has also demonstrated, a new idea of God (Gilson, 1930, pp. 224-233). Yet all this innovation is to be effected by the graduate of a Jesuit college, who, if he had abandoned books to read the book of the world, nevertheless approached his enterprise in physics, and then in metaphysics, with a mind-set formed by his teachers and attuned to the criticisms, as well as the praise, of contemporaries who had been schooled, if not in the same, then in other variants of the scholastic tradition.

He welcomed responses to the *Discourse* and its accompanying essays, and of course took pains to look for, and reply to, objections to the *Meditations* before their publication. If, as he confessed to Mersenne, he hoped his readers would shed their Aristotelianism without noticing that they had done so (AT III, 298), he was nevertheless speaking to them as a man of their time, whose thought had been formed in their tradition and still showed in many of its aspects the mark of that formation. He was a consummate borer from within. It is significant that when, after long residence in the Netherlands, a friend requested advice on the education of his son, Descartes recommended La Flèche (AT II, 378). It is significant also that he expressed special concern for the opinion of the Society of Jesus about his work, sending the *Discourse* to Father Noël at La Flèche (AT I, 383), rejoicing in its kind reception by one Father Vatier (AT I, 558 ff; cf. letter to Huygens, AT II, 50), and worrying lest the carping criticism of another Jesuit priest, Bourdin, might express the misunderstanding of the Order itself (AT III, 280-1, 523). And of course, strange as it may appear to us, he seems to have hoped that his *Principles* would be adopted as a text in the schools, presumably including those of his former teachers (III, 276, VII, 577).

The *Principles* were published in 1644. As far back as 1637, when he published his first major work, Descartes appeared to some of his readers at least to be working within, or better, perhaps, to be thoroughly familiar with, the realm of scholastic discourse. After his first exchange with J.-B. Morin, a rather stuffy professor of mathematics at Paris, Mersenne addressed him (in a marginal note, apparently to a lost letter) with great enthusiasm:

> You have so much consoled and enriched us by the excellent replies that you have made to M. Morin and me, that I assure you that instead of the 38 *sous* (pence?) postage charged on the packet, seeing what it contained, I would willingly have paid 38 *écus* (sovereigns?). We read your reply together, and M. Morin found your style so excellent, that I advise you never to change it . . . . For the rest, you have made a great hit in your reply to M. Morin by showing that you do not despise, or at least you are

> not ignorant of, the Philosophy of Aristotle.
> That is what has contributed to increasing
> the esteem that M. Morin declares he has
> for you . . . (AT II, 287).

The correspondence soon went sour, but the point is that Descartes did not by any means appear to all his readers as a radical innovator (cf. Garber, 1988).

So far I have just been reformulating and supporting Gilson's Cartesian thesis. Like any substantive historical hypothesis, however, the notion of Descartes's retention of scholastic doctrines and concepts has turned out to be more complicated than it may have looked at first, at least to outsiders like myself who lack intimate knowledge of the subtleties of scholastic debate. If Descartes is a more traditional thinker than many of his readers have supposed, that tradition itself resists simple or uniform characterization. Descartes was trained by Jesuits; Jesuits were instructed to follow St. Thomas in theology and Aristotle in philosophy. It seems to follow that the scholastic influence in Descartes's case is Thomistic. He did say that, though not a bookish thinker, he had a *Summa* as well as a Bible with him in Holland (AT II, 630). That seems all very straightforward. Or is it? Let me make, briefly and sketchily, two points that cast doubt on this simple inference.

First, the Jesuits of La Flèche were no run-of-the-mill purveyors of St. Thomas's texts. In the time of the Counter-Reformation, they were in the vanguard of advanced and sophisticated thought. In particular, they were learned in recent work in mathematics and concerned with experimental techniques and the role of mathematics in experiment. Although I don't want to burden you by specifying my sources at every step, I must mention here in particular the work of Peter Dear on mathematics and experiment in the Society of Jesus (Dear, 1987). Granted, as far back as Gilson's *Index* of Cartesian scholastic sources, it has been clear that the Thomism of Descartes's teachers was invigorated by their use of philosophers like Suarez or commentators like the Coimbrans. But recent work such as that of Dear has shown Jesuit mathematical and scientific practice in the seventeenth century to be astonishingly diverse and astonishingly innovative, if within the limits allowed by the tradition. Descartes, in his insistence on the total novelty of his enterprise, often confirms the common conception of the "School" he is opposing as a dried-up monolithic bunch of word-mongers. But his teachers, and their confreres later in the century, were much more sophisticated and much more in touch with the avantgarde of then contemporary thought than such tirades would lead us to believe.

If Descartes's Jesuit teachers were obliged to teach Thomism, moreover – and this is my second point – it was not, it seems, a pure Thomism that was conveyed to their pupils. There were clearly non-Thomist threads of thought that could well make their way into the conceptual apparatus of those who studied with them, like René Descartes or Marin Mersenne (cf. Ariew, 1991a,b). Descartes's first argument for God, for instance, relies heavily on his peculiar use of the concept of "objective" as against formal reality. Until Tom Prendergast pointed out to me, a few years ago, that this is by no means Thomistic usage, I had simply taken "objective" in Descartes's sense as part of his scholastic baggage. Well, it is and it isn't. Gilson, in his edition of the *Discourse* in 1926, stressed the non-Thomist character of this argument and of the conceptual units employed in it (Gilson, 1926). Recently my colleague Roger Ariew called my attention to a paper by one R. Dalbiez, published in 1929, in which the intrusion of Scotist and other non-Thomist elements into Descartes's "scholasticism" are cunningly explained (Dalbiez, 1929).[1]

Dalbiez makes two major points. First, the Roman edition of the works of St. Thomas, published in 1570-1571 by order of Pius V, contains the commentaries of Cajetan on the *Summa*. Now, as Dalbiez carefully shows, Cajetan deals in some detail with Scotus's conception of objective reality, contrasting it with that of the Angelic Doctor. What Scotus really meant may remain controversial, but this much is plain: instead of considering objective being a mere *ens rationis*, he does accord it some degree of reality, and he also associates with such "objective beings" the term "idea" – a thoroughly Cartesian usage. True, as Gilson and Dalbiez agree, no one before Descartes had constructed out of these concepts his peculiar causal argument. But the source in scholasticism for the material he uses is surely clear enough.

In addition, Dalbiez points out, there was controversy about the role of "objective being" in the definition of truth in Jesuit philosophy: between Suarez and Vasquez in particular. It all begins with one Durand of Saint-Pourçain, whom Suarez attacks in the first section of his *Disputatio metaphysica*. As reported by Suarez:

> [His] first proposition is, that [formal] truth resides, not in the formal act or knowledge of the intellect, but in the thing known as objective in (*objecta* – thrown into?) the intellect, so that it [i.e. the thing] is in conformity with itself from the side of the existent thing, and in this way he explains that truth is the conformity of the intellect to the thing, that is, it is the conformity of the objective concept of the disclosing intellect

to the thing according to its real being (Dalbiez, 1929, p. 408).

Suarez, predictably, attacks this account of truth, with its interposition of a third reality between thought and thing, but another Jesuit commentator, Vasquez, in turn defends Durand. Dalbiez concludes, very reasonably:

Descartes could not have been wholly ignorant of this discussion. Whether his professor of philosophy was a partisan of Suarez or of Vasquez, he could not neglect the exposition of a controversy that divided two of the most celebrated doctors of the Society (Dalbiez, 1929, pp. 469-470).

In short, a study of the literature that must have been current among Descartes's teachers, and conveyed to their pupils, reveals the complexity and subtlety of Descartes's scholastic roots. If he disavowed the learning of the School, he seems to have held at the back of his mind a rather mixed conceptual apparatus, derived from a variety of scholastic sources, on which he depends in a pretty complicated way when he comes to construct what appeared to him and, eventually, to many others a radically innovative metaphysic as the foundation for a radically innovative physics (and eventually, he hoped, mechanics, morality and medicine).

Before I go on to discuss one particular example of Descartes's retention of a scholastic concept, the case of substantial forms, and the peculiar use he made of it, let me add, very briefly, that not only Scotist, but more sweepingly Augustinian themes may well have formed another strand in the web of Cartesian thought. For the seventeenth century in general Gouhier's magisterial work on Cartesianism and Augustinianism must be referred to here (Gouhier, 1978). That Descartes resuscitated Augustinian themes, especially in the *cogito*, everybody knows, and noticed from the beginning. Whether he really reinvented this particular wheel, or borrowed it, I don't suppose any one knows or ever will know. It doesn't matter much. The point is that, like Scotism in particular, Augustinian tendencies in general were always somewhere in the background in scholastic debate. Dear's **Mersenne and the Learning of the Schools** (Dear, 1988) makes this clear for the case of the Minim. That an Augustinian admixture may also have adhered to the scholastic teaching half-remembered, if half-forgotten, by Descartes, also seems probable – even apart from the possible influence of Cardinal Bérulle and the Oratory during Descartes's years in Paris in the 1620's. Admittedly, this is conjecture, but an attempt at historical reconstruction can never hope to attain pure Cartesian evidence.

Taking as given, then, the depth and complexity of Descartes's scholastic heritage, I want now to consider a single example from this rich store: the case of substantial forms. Real qualities go along with these; Descartes seems seldom to separate the two concepts. As I noted in passing earlier, this case is especially significant in the light it sheds on the relation between Descartes's physics and its metaphysical foundation. When he became interested in constructing a new physics, he happily rejected substantial forms and real qualities in favor of what seemed a better, because simpler, mechanical explanation of natural phenomena. But when he needed to ground that physics in a metaphysic, there was a special case of substantial form he invoked to explain the activity of the whole human being, mind and body together, in this life.

First, let's look at the texts in which he uses, or refers to, these concepts, especially substantial form and allied locutions [Table One]. Then I want to compare the more or less Aristotelian conception with the Cartesian, try to imagine how Descartes might have arrived at his transformation of the traditional notion, and finally, notice how he had to transform the concept of substance itself in order to establish his new ontology.

First, then, the texts. Starting from Gilson's Index, I have added a few other passages in which, although the same terms are not used, the same points are being made. Although I am not assuming that my list is complete, I confess I wish it were, since as it stands it provides such a neat contrast between two sets of cases.

Table One
Texts concerned with substantial form

Substantial forms as such:
AT I, 243: will keep some substantial forms.
    II, 74: away with forms and qualities!
    II, 200: their explanatory principles (i.e., real qualities, substantial forms) almost infinite; I say only that bodies consist of parts.
    II, 223: vs. explanation of weight through form and matter.
    II, 362: substantial form of sun "a philosophical being unknown to me."
    II, 485: because of subtle matter, no matter that can't take on successively all forms.
    III, 212: substantial forms are chimaeras.
    III, 197-8: *Meditations* destroy principles of Aristotle.
    III, 420: substantial forms invented through confusion of bodily and mental.
    III, 435: form/matter/accident not a real distinction.

III, 492, 500-503: to Regius: misunderstandings to be avoided (Even if there are substantial forms, they're unnecessary).

III, 528: everybody laughs at substantial forms.

III, 648: no real qualities in my physics.

III, 667: real qualities unnecessary.

III, 694: weight and real quality.

VI, 239: *Meteorology*: doesn't deny substantial form and real quality, just doesn't need them.

VII, 441-443: away with substantial form (weight)!

VIII, 1, 322: substantial form unnecessary for explanation of movement.

XI, 7: against explanation of movement through forms, etc.

Substantial forms in human case:

II, 353, 496: individual one in number.

II, 477-8: God could unite closely two separate substances.

III, 460: human being *ens per se* and *ens per accidens*.

III, 493, 503: substantial form only in the case of man.

III, 665-6: the three primitive notions.

III, 691: the three primitive notions.

IV, 164-9: unity of human individual.

IV, 166: contrast with animals.

IV, 346: individual one because of form, which
is the soul.

V, 163: conversation with Burman: unity of man
very hard to explain, but undeniable on
the ground of experience.

V, 166 ff.: soul in whole body.

V, 222-3: unity of man one of the things known
in itself.

VII, 81: 6th Meditation.

VII, 219-228: 4th Replies, esp. 219, 222, 228:
substantial unity.

VII, 6th Replies, esp. 424, 435, 444: same point.

VIII, 1, 315: reference to human soul "although
it informs the whole body" (*informare*).

VIII, 2, 347-352, esp. 350-1: *ens per se*
(simple and compound substances).

X, 411: soul as form of body.

XI, 351: soul joined to whole body.

Just look! We have nineteen texts concerned
with substantial forms or real qualities as such,
and another nineteen dealing in particular with
the unity of man, usually in terms of the concept
of form or substantial form or substantial unity. If
it seems strange to balance the general against the
particular – substantial forms in general vs. substantial forms in the human case – the reason for
this arrangement is simple: most of the general
passages attack substantial forms one way or

another; most of the passages referring to mankind only support the doctrine. Substantial forms must go – but not in our case.[2]

Let me take up briefly some of the passages I have listed. Among the first nineteen, three do not in fact deny substantial forms and real qualities directly. At AT I, 243 Descartes writes to Mersenne, that he will keep some substantial forms in *Le Monde* (although according to the last text in this list he doesn't seem to have done so!). At AT III, 492 he reminds Regius that in the *Meteors* he had not denied substantial forms, but had only remarked that they were not necessary for his explanations (he is referring to the passage in AT VI, 239). Of course this remark may well be a political one: one doesn't want to offend the School unless it's really necessary. In any case, we have only sixteen texts that are directed explicitly against the scholastic terminology, and in contrast we have nineteen speaking expressly for the unity of man, a unity that is best articulated in the language of scholasticism, that is, through the concept of substantial form. So in effect it's sixteen against and nineteen for.

Typical for the first group, for example, is the assertion that the substantial form of the sun is "a philosophical entity unknown to me": *"un être philosophique qui m'est inconnu"* (AT II, 362), or the statement that substantial forms are chimaeras

(AT III, 212). On the other side, for instance in the long letter to Regius from which I've already quoted (AT III, 491 ff.) the fact is positively celebrated that the human soul is a substantial form, and indeed the only one there is. In another letter (AT IV, 346) Descartes speaks of the human individual, which is one "because of the form, which is the soul." Moreover, in the Twelfth Rule, and thus in the 1620's, and again in the *Principles*, almost twenty years later, the scholastic verb *informare*, to give form to, is used to describe the relation of soul and body (AT X, 411, VIII, 315). This seems to me a most significant retention of a deeply Aristotelian concept. In other words, substantial forms, like real qualities, are banished everywhere from nature, only not in the case of the human being. Nor can this be simply hypocrisy or politics, since the assertions in the letters, not only in published works, are too emphatic to be thus easily dismissed. We must take Descartes's teaching here quite seriously: there is in all the world only one substantial form, ours, but that one there undeniably is.

Before we ask how he might have arrived at such a view, let us compare briefly Descartes's view of the place of man in nature as suggested by our passages – as well of course as by the doctrine of his major published works – with that of Aristotle himself and then of seventeenth century

Aristotelians, or more generally, of the Aristotelian tradition.

In Aristotelian nature hylomorphism prevails almost everywhere. Paradigmatic for substance are above all living things. Everywhere in the world we find three great levels of organization, plants, animals (other than human beings) and people. Every level consists of material beings which are *informed* by functions which can be called *souls*. The matter-form analysis can then be extrapolated to other, non-living substances. For everything that exists under the moon, it is essential, on the one hand that form and matter always exist together: every form is embodied and all matter can exist only as informed, and on the other hand it is equally essential that form has ontological priority. Aristotle declares in Book Theta of the *Metaphysics*: matter is potentially, in order that it may come into form, and when it is actual, it is in the form (*Met* 1050 a 15-16). This intimate coexistence between form and matter, or in the case of living things between soul and body, has, however, *one* exception. In the case of human beings, it appears, *nous*, active intellect, comes from elsewhere. Although in the fifth chapter of book III of the *De Anima* this may not be wholly clear, we cannot argue away the text of the *De Generatione Animalium*: *nous*, and *nous* alone, comes "from elsewhere" and is divine (*De Gen*

Anim 736 b 28-9). Everywhere else the insight of the great biologist prevails: it is a question of the many-levelled, many-sided organization of matter, differentiated in many different ways, a matter that never occurs as matter only, but only within the domination of some form or other, some style of organization. In this vision of nature, *nous*, which occurs on the whole earth only in the case of human beings (perhaps only adult male human beings?), presents a strange exception.

With Descartes, too, man constitutes an exception, but in just the opposite direction. Descartes abolished the natural unity of form and matter. All that was for him excess baggage, which the scholastics, with their childish, prejudice-laden thought style, had simply invented. If we can only overcome our childish trust in the senses as well as our trust in the terminology invented by our teachers, he believed, we can win through to the clear and distinct insight that the whole of nature consists of pure *res extensae*, things stretched out in space. The objects of pure geometry, which for the tradition and its originator are mere abstractions, now remain as the only substances existing in the natural world. In Cartesian physics the concept of an ensouled body appears confused and misleading.

Yet in this whole desert, on the one single plane to which the rich, many-levelled nature of tradition has been reduced, there is nevertheless, according to Descartes, still *one* case of the unity of form and matter: that of the ensouled body of man. In nature as such Descartes sharply separated matter from form or body from soul. There are no longer any forms, any souls in nature. But our souls, like *nous* in Aristotle, seem to come from elsewhere. They are certainly not natural! Yet in contrast to active mind in Aristotle, *mens* in Descartes no longer forms an exception in an otherwise hylomorphic nature. For it is not the separateness of mind from merely material things, the duality of body and soul, that now appears exceptional. On the contrary: in contrast to the splintering of nature, where only extended, purely geometrical, entities (unsouled machines!) prevail, there remains for man, and only for man, the old unity of form and matter or soul and body. This single surviving substantial form, it appears, has the power to produce a unity out of two independent substances, the unity that *is* this or that existing human being. This form, in its unity with the body that it informs: this is the exception, which sets up in nature, or against nature, a singular contrast or even contradiction.

Like many readers of Aristotle, I find the separateness of active intellect hard to swallow; I leave that to Aristotelian scholars to interpret. But if *nous* is tough, the strange, exceptional unity of Cartesian man is harder yet. No wonder Descartes told Princess Elizabeth it was difficult to understand at the same time the separation of mind and body and their intimate, this-worldly union (AT III, 693). Yet we have to make a stab at it, for after all his belaboring of the real distinction in the **Meditations** there *is*, we are told in the Sixth Meditation, presumably at the culmination of the argument, that unity more intimate than that of a sailor with his ship (in the French translation, a pilot) (AT VII, 81; IX, 1, 64). And there are also all those passages insisting on the human soul (the only finite spiritual substance that there is, of course) as being in fact the substantial form of its body.

In this impasse, let's look again at the Aristotelian or scholastic model on which the traditional view of nature rested, and let us consider, on the basis of our Cartesian texts, how Descartes must have reread this model, in order to arrive at his rejection of substantial forms in every case but ours. Finally we will consider how the concept of substance is itself transformed by this rereading.

In scholasticism in general, as for Aristotle, the organism seems to be paradigmatic for substance. But in the case of organisms what is especially striking is the phenomenon of birth and death, *genesis* and *phthora*. Living things come into being and pass away. Indeed, that is why the concept of substantial form is needed: for when a new substance is born, a new form thereby comes to exist, which characterizes that substance. Aristotle is a bit hard to pin down on this; the invention by his heirs of the concept of "substantial form" makes explicit the point he seems to be making, for instance, in the dialectical argument of Book One of the *Physics*. The use of this concept fixes, not just the priority of form over matter, but the priority of substantial change over other forms of alteration, that is, over accidental change, whether of quality, size or place. When people look around their world, after all, it is the renewal and at the same time the ephemeral quality of life that strikes them: plants sprout and wither, animals are born and die. Life's coming and going is the first phenomenon to be described and explained. That is how Gilson interpreted the motivation for the concept of substantial form, an interpretation that I find entirely convincing (Gilson, 1930, p. 154). According to Descartes, indeed, the philosophy of the School was in fact the philosophy of every day, the philosophy of common sense. We start with life, and with the primary circumstance of life: with birth and death.

How does Descartes interpret this doctrine? The form that must come into being along with any given matter he simply does not see at all. He overlooks the phenomenon of life from the beginning. Instead he tells an entirely different story. As children, misled by our senses, we all believed that much, for instance, color, sound, heat, pain, exists in the world, which in fact occurs only subjectively, in our feelings rather than out there. The scholastics in their naivete have retained this belief even as adults and have passed it on to their unfortunate pupils. Thus they attribute to the external world much that really belongs to the province of the soul. They talk about substantial forms and real qualities, that is, as Descartes sees it, about little souls, which they confusedly ascribe to bodies: "which are added to substance, like little souls to their bodies," as he puts it (AT III, 648).

His favorite example is *gravitas*, weight (e.g. AT III, 694; also, in another context, AT VII, 219-228 and 441-3). In the Sixth Replies, for instance, he reconstructs, from his more mature and enlightened perspective, how as child and youth he must have arrived at this concept. Tied to the senses, he always formed a material image even of intellectual things. Although he always had the ideas of soul and body as separate, he thus confused them with one another: as he says, "he took the one and the other for the same thing – he related to body all the notions he had of intellectual matters." So long as he had not freed himself from these prejudices, he would not have known anything with sufficient distinctness not to consider it as somehow material, although – and this is important for us – "nevertheless," he writes, "I often formed such ideas of the very things that I supposed to be bodily, and had such notions of them, that they referred rather to minds than to bodies" (AT VII,441). Then we have the beloved example of weight. Although he understood weight as a quality of the body, at the same time he took it to be a *real* quality, that is, in effect a substance, which inhabits every little part of the body, as the mind does every part of our body. But that means that it is an analogy with mind that suggests the very concept of real qualities, and *a fortiori* that of the substantial forms allied to them. One feature makes it especially evident to Descartes that the idea of weight stems partly from his idea of mind: namely, as he says, "that I thought heaviness led bodies to the center of the earth, as if it had in itself some knowledge of that center: for certainly it is not possible that this should happen without knowledge, and there is no knowledge without mind" (AT VII, 442). But on the other hand he also ascribed to weight or heaviness material properties like divisibility, measurability and so on. In a letter, probably to the Abbé de Launay, he insists, again, that we have invented substantial forms through confusing mind and body (AT III, 420-421). We have somehow attached "little souls" to extended things, and, as his readers know from the Second Meditation, we have thought of ourselves, though we are really thinking things, as bodily. Even if we thought about the soul, we constantly invoked imagination in the form of bodily images. I thought of the soul, says the meditator, as "something extremely rare and subtle, as a wind, a flame or a very thin air, which crept into and spread through my grosser parts" (AT VII, 26). What concerns us here, however, is not so much the materialization of mind as the mentalization of body, if I may so call it. Real qualities and substantial forms are supposed to have been invented through the extrapolation of the intellectual to the merely extended. Instead of starting out from life, from the manifold styles of organization that we find in the world around us: sprouting, ripening and withering of plants, birth, growth and death of animals: instead of being impressed by the regularity and richness of nature, which every human being sees around him, we are supposed, according to Descartes, to have started from a confusing mixture of the purely intellectual with the purely extended, and thus from two rather *recherché* abstractions, which we have learned to distinguish clearly and distinctly only through our Cartesian liberation from the senses. Only now can we understand how we had earlier confused what is to be clearly distinguished. And so we can explain how we invented the concept of the living, of the organization of animal life through its operating principles, or "souls," by illicitly applying to body what really belongs to mind.

From the perspective of the Aristotelian tradition, this is just downright nonsense. Soul in general, let alone form in general, can by no means be identified with intellect. On the contrary, as I have been saying over and over, it is life, the unity of form and matter, that gives us the model to start from if we want to explain the wealth and plurality of nature. Mind must be explained as one remarkable, unique kind of soul, and not, as with Descartes, all of nature explained as a distorted mirroring of mind.

Now surely Descartes must have been by far the cleverest pupil that the masters of La Flèche ever had the pleasure of instructing. How can he have misunderstood them so wildly? As we have been insisting, he retains a great deal from his scholastic training. Yet the very core of his teachers' ontology he turns into nonsense. Why?

To answer this question, we must try, if only very sketchily – and much more monolithically than recent scholarship suggests (see Bibliographical Note) – to reconstruct the course of development of Cartesian physics (and metaphysics), and then to elicit from this some oddities of Descartes's concept of substance.

Formed, willy nilly, by his teachers' scholastic thought style, the young Descartes, in that famous winter night of 1619, experiences the dream, or the vision, that will govern his intellectual life from that moment on. That this overwhelming vision has something to do with his method seems clear. He tries to apply this method to begin with for the construction of a new physics, which will explain all the phenomena of nature mathematically, and so more economically than the antiquated physics of the Aristotelians. The *Rules*, though fragmentary and apparently composed at different times, sketch a path for that new way. At the very beginning of this document, in the explanation of the First Rule, the sharp contrast of the intellectual from the bodily is already emphasized: wisdom is everywhere indivisible; bodily skill, in contrast, can only be developed in some specialized way in one direction or another. Method must begin with the liberation of mind (AT X, 359-361). Even though with due caution we can later use imagination and perception in science, it is first and last a "pure and attentive mind" that must initiate and carry out the precepts of method. On the other side, nature, that is, matter, can be made intelligible through the clear concepts of such an intellect, in the first instance through the concepts of the geometer, in a new, simpler, more accurate fashion. Thus the dualism of the mature Descartes lies at the foundation even of this early work. However the "method" changed, or even if, as Garber argues, it was abandoned (Garber, 1991) – in favor of what? but that's another story – in short, however he changed his view of his own enterprise, Descartes held fast to the separation of intellect, which is one, and matter, which is always divided and divisible.

If we set intellect free to explain extended things, however, we can describe nature directly as geometers with the help of mathematical concepts like magnitude, divisibility and local motion, that is, in terms of displacement in Euclidean space. But then all the complex scholastic so-called explanations simply drop out.

Yet the elaboration of the new natural science was not so simple. In 1629-30 Descartes seems to have decided that his new physics needed a (partly?) new metaphysic. He had to distinguish clearly and distinctly thinking substance from extended substance, and also to ground the knowledge of the latter by the former firmly in the veracity of God. He made this program public only in the **Meditations** of 1641. However, as far as nature goes, he had made a sketch of the new view in the early thirties in **Le Monde**, a project that he abandoned because of the condemnation of Galileo. And in the **Dioptrics** he showed through a significant example how questions of natural philosophy could be handled from the new perspective. All change becomes local motion, which can be mechanistically explained. The meaningless forms and qualities of the scholastics have become simply superfluous. Away with the lot!

Now if we have made the foundation of our thought this great discovery: that is, on the one hand the real distinction, the basic independence of mind from body, and on the other the reduction of nature to extension and thus the reduction of all natural change to local motion, how are we to explain the fact that so many scholars still believe in the old fairy tale of form and quality? As we have seen, we have to remember the natural errors of childhood, and then we can imagine how children and naive adults could believe that non-human bodies, which are really just pieces of extension, somehow have little souls added to them, which somehow direct their movements. (Of course our body-machines do have such souls attached; we know that directly, but we have no reason to extrapolate from this to other cases.)

In this situation, what has become of the human soul, which is the substantial form of the human body? *Nothing at all has happened to it;* that's what is so remarkable. This one form, as hard to explain as it is undeniable in our daily experience, this one form survives, all alone, in splendid isolation, the disappearance from reality of all its kin. How is that possible? Mind and body are two; the real distinction is real. How can these two substances be transformed, through the operation of the substantial form that is the soul, into one substance, or at least into a "substantial unity"?

The answer is twofold. First, as I have argued, following Gilson and more recent interpreters in the same tradition, we must never forget that Descartes wanted to alter in the tradition only as much as was needed for the establishment of a mathematical physics. To this end, as we've seen, substantial forms and real qualities had to be withdrawn from nature. Yet man remains in this life intimately and firmly bound to his body. Even if our body, as body, like that of brutes, becomes a pure machine, which is to be explained wholly through the concept of extension and the laws of motion and impetus, nevertheless the unity of mind and body remains in our case, different as it is from that of the non-feeling, because non-thinking, *bêtes machines*. In our case, one substance is mysteriously (*arctissime*, says Descartes; AT VII, 81) composed of two. This insight of the school, the third "common notion" of the letter to Elizabeth, the loyal pupil of La Flèche, the good Catholic, never for a moment denied, much less the man René Descartes, who, like all human beings, felt pain, hunger, passion. He set it aside in the First Meditation, and, especially in the second, even seemed to be denying it. Yet despite the stress on dualism, it turns up again undamaged in the Sixth. As possessors of clear and distinct ideas we know of the duality of mind and body; yet as living human beings we always experience, always feel at first hand, the intimate unity of body and soul, which remains – for all the rubbish we've thrown out in our seemingly radical job of intellectual housecleaning firmly in place at the end of the last meditation as it was before the beginning of the first. Isn't that what meditations are for? We are supposed, through them, to cleanse and purify ourselves; yet it is still ourselves, flesh and spirit, mind in body, that we are, at the close as before the beginning of our exercise. Better, we hope, but still ourselves (cf. Hatfield, 1986).

The question was, however, how could the two substances of the real distinction form one substance, or, strictly speaking, a substantial unity? The first part of my answer consisted in a reaffirmation of the Gilson thesis: this was something Descartes retained from his scholastic education, as he did so much else. Indeed, mind-body unity in this life would have been fundamental to the construction of all three offshoots of his metaphysic, had he lived to develop them. As the introduction to the French version of the *Principles* enumerates them, these were to be: mechanics (as Descartes interprets it, a practical science, the craft of building and using various mechanical devices), morality (the art of controlling the passions, which, though attributed to the soul, arise from its union with the body) and medicine, in which mind would have developed techniques for prolonging the existence of its bodily machine, techniques obviously needed only in this life, while mind and body are so intimately joined together.

But now my answer leads to a more difficult problem. How has Descartes, despite the traditional ontological maxims he clings to, transformed the foundational concept of the tradition, the concept of substance itself, so as to construct his new, and in many ways antischolastic, world, including all three, a formless nature, a disembodiable mind and a unified mind-body? That is my last point: the alteration, and indeed impoverishment, of the concept of substance in Descartes. How is this transformation to be understood, which retains the concept of the unity of man despite, or even because of, its radical dualism?

Obviously, Descartes remains at bottom a substance metaphysician. When critics complain that in a nature consisting wholly of extension, the "substance" of bodies seems to vanish, Descartes replies, succinctly and peevishly, that everybody knows the difference between substance and attribute (AT V, 70-71). But what *is* Cartesian substance? In my little book on Descartes I included a chapter called "Substance at Risk," in which I tried to enumerate the ways in which the concept of substance in Descartes was emaciated and even endangered (Grene, 1985). Think for instance of the thesis that every substance has only one attribute, or of the restriction of levels of reality to three: one infinite substance, two kinds of finite substance and finally their modes. Or recall how difficult it is to count Cartesian bodies or to ascribe to them any kind of development. But here I want to stress two further characteristics of Cartesian substance, which I overlooked in that discussion. For the recognition of the first of these, which is directly connected with the problem of the unity of man, I am indebted to Paul Hoffman's paper on this question (Hoffman, 1986); in fact, it was Hoffman's essay that started me thinking about this question at all. The second follows, as I see it, directly from the first.

Descartes defines substance (meaning here, of course, primarily finite substance) sometimes as the subject of properties, sometimes as that which needs only the power of God in order to exist, sometimes as that which can be in itself, that is, which exists independently (insofar as that is possible for a finite being). From such formulae Hoffman draws a remarkable inference. From the fact that a substance is the bearer of properties, for instance, one cannot exclude the possibility that a substance *could* occur as the property of another substance. Or if we understand substance as that which can exist on its own, it does not follow that a finite substance must always in fact exist so independently. The definition presents *a possibility*, not a fact that must obtain at all times, under all circumstances. Descartes does explicitly (e.g. AT VIII b, 350-1) distinguish between simple and complex substances, the latter consisting of more than one substance. According to him, we can take a man and his suit, for example, as two substances, or we can count the man and his suit as one substance, namely, as a man who has the property of being dressed in such and such a way. Or we can count a hand as a substance, as well as the body it belongs to; but equally well we can take the whole body as one substance, to which this hand belongs as part, or mode. And in such complex substances, it seems that one of the substances serves as accident or mode of the other.

As a theory of substance this is surely very odd. Yet it fits perfectly with the Cartesian view of human unity. For in this way we can understand very well the metaphor of the soul's being more than sailor (or pilot) in the body. Body is substance, but a body can sometimes belong to a mind as its accident – and supposedly vice versa – although if the mind is the form of the body, the body cannot really, conversely, be the form of mind, and so the mind its accident. Yet how can one understand reality in terms of substance and consider a substance as a possible mode, and thus a non-substance? Nevertheless, I am now convinced, that is precisely what Descartes does. To do this, however, he had to abandon a fundamental axiom of the tradition, an axiom perhaps not explicitly stated, yet still foundational. (This is the second point I want to add to my recounting of Descartes's transformation of substance metaphysic.) I mean the principle that everything there is is unambiguously and ineradicably *either* substance *or* accident of a substance – and not both, not even under different circumstances. Substance is substance, accident is accident. This principle is not to be circumvented. But Descartes overthrew it. No wonder, then, that after him traditional substance metaphysic fell into such confusion. We could also notice here, if we liked, the Aristotelian distinction between accidents and parts, which Descartes seems to overlook. That is a subtle problem, which I cannot here pursue. My point is just this: that Descartes could save the unity of man in the face of his sharp dualism, only through the radical impairment of the concept of substance itself. Only Spinoza on the one hand, Hume on the other, seem to offer ways of escape that can overcome the weakness of the Cartesian compromise.

Endnotes

1. Gilson in fact refers to this article in a footnote in his 1930 essays (Gilson, 1930, p. 204), and admits in the text that these concepts, though non-Thomistic, are nevertheless scholastic. Were I a specialist in scholastic philosophy, I might also adduce here Wells's paper on "Objective Being: Descartes and his Sources" (Wells, 1967), as well as his recent essay, "Objective Reality of Ideas in Descartes, Caterus and Suarez" (Wells, 1990), but Dalbiez's exposition is simpler, and so, for me, clearer.

2. Roger Ariew argues that since the anti-substantial-form references are relatively early and the pro-substantial-form-in-our-case passages relatively late, Descartes only conceived of the human case late and as an afterthought (Ariew, pers. comm.). I would suggest, on the contrary, that if one wants to take the internal evidence this way, one must also say, improbably if not absurdly, that after the years covered by AT I-III, Descartes abandoned his opposition to substantial forms in general, since he doesn't any longer go on about them. It seems to me more reasonable to suppose that, although he wished to exorcise those concepts for the sake of his physics, he needed to modify his abolition of them for metaphysical purposesd indeed, to establish the subject matter of the three branches of his tree of knowledge – and so dredged up the hylomorphic view of man in this life from the store of scholastic notions he always had around somewhere if he needed them. For my general scepticism about periodization based on internal evidence only, see the bibliographical note below.

Bibliographical Note

Cartesian scholarship has been enriched in the last decade or more in a number of directions. Without venturing to provide more than a very partial guide to the riches fast becoming available here, let me point out three kinds of study proliferating in the recent literature.

In part, there is a growing literature that illuminates the texts themselves (for there are texts themselves!) with special clarity and insight. Garber (1986) and Curley (1986), which I mentioned in passing, belong to this group: they help us understand with new depth the aim of the *Meditations* and thus the articulation of Descartes's argument. Curley's essay together with Rodis-Lewis's contribution to the same collection (Rodis-Lewis, 1986 in Rorty, ed., 1986), moreover, suggest a new reading of the place of the third proof of God in relation to the first two that demands a rethinking of the whole structure of the work. The essay by Hoffman (Hoffman, 1986) from which the second part of my lecture takes its start, again, provides an excellent example of very careful reading that guides the student to an aspect of Cartesian philosophy usually overlooked. On Cartesian physics as well as metaphysics, Gaukroger's anthology (Gaukroger, ed.,

1982) broke new ground, and work by such scholars as Garber and Hatfield (Garber, 1991; Hatfield, e.g., 1985, 1988) have continued to good effect the exploration of Cartesian science.

Some work, further, puts the Cartesian philosophy, or particular Cartesian texts, into the context of the literature of the time. Hatfield's contribution to the Rorty volume places the *Meditations* within their literary genre and so helps us read them in the proper spirit: not as formal argument but as intellectual therapy. More broadly, works like that of Marion (1981) place Descartes's thought intimately into relation to the philosophy of his scholastic predecessors, and Gouhier (1978), which I mentioned in passing, illuminates one aspect of Descartes's relation to the tradition: the connections between Cartesian and Augustinian philosophy. Ariew's essay on Descartes and scholasticism in the forthcoming *Cambridge Companion to Descartes* provides an important survey of Descartes's scholastic education and (in Ariew's view) reeducation in his mature period (Ariew, 1991b). The treatment of Jesuit education is particularly illuminating, especially together with Dear's study of Jesuit mathematics (Dear, 1987). Dear's work on Mersenne (Dear, 1988), while not directly concerned with Descartes, adds immeasurably to the student's sense of the intellectual milieu in which he worked, as does Brockliss's detailed study of French college and university education in this period (Brockliss, 1987). For all this work, students of Descartes can only be deeply grateful.

There is a third aspect of such recent work that may well be equally significant, although I confess to some unease about it. That is the interpretation, through his works and letters, of Descartes's development. Since, when I was a student, the fashionable approach to Kant was through the Vaihinger-Kemp Smith reading, which subdivided the First Critique by periods within periods, and since I also remember well the Jaeger era in Aristotelian scholarship or the days when everybody had to show that Plato ultimately became a Wittgensteinian, I am leery of readings of development based on internal evidence. It was, I suppose, Weber's analysis of the *Rules* that set off this fashion for Descartes (Weber, 1964; see Schuster, 1982 or Garber, 1991 for examples of this style of exposition). And of course it is clear, since they were left incompleted, that something about the *Rules* turned out to be unsatisfactory. But to go back to the patchwork gambit seems to me regrettable, and to argue that Descartes abandoned any conception of method leaves me gasping. However, there it all is; for Descartes's natural philosophy Garber (1991) is perhaps the most massive example so far of this historiographic style.

The following bibliography includes items referred to in my text, as well as titles illustrative of the recent scholarship I have been discussing. It makes no claim to completeness, but is meant to guide the reader who wishes to explore the field a little further.

Bibliography

All references to Descartes are by volume and page of the Adam and Tannery edition (C. Adam and P. Tannery, eds., *Oeuvres de Descartes*, new edition, Paris: Vrin, 1973-6), as e.g. AT II, 630. Translations are my own.

Other references:

Ariew, R. 1991a. "Body and the Physical World." Part IV, ch. 1 in *Cambridge History of Seventeenth Century Philosophy*. Cambridge: Cambridge University Press.

Ariew, R. 1991b. "Descartes and Scholasticism." In J. Cottingham, ed., *Cambridge Companion to Descartes*.

Brockliss, L.W.B. 1987. *French Higher Education in the Seventeenth and Eighteenth Centuries*. Oxford: Clarendon Press.

Curley, E.M. 1986. "Analysis in the Meditations: The Quest for Clear and Distinct Ideas." In: A. Rorty, ed., *Essays on Descartes's Meditations*. Berkeley and Los Angeles: University of California Press, pp. 153-176.

Dalbiez, R. 1919. "Les sources scolastiques de la théorie cartésienne de l'être objectif (à propos du Descartes de M. Gilson)." *Revue d'histoire de la philosophie*. III: 464-472.

Dear, P. 1987. "Jesuit Mathematical Science and the Reconstitution of Experience in the Early Seventeenth Century." *Stud. Hist. Phil. Sci.* 18: 133-175.

Dear, P. 1988. *Mersenne and the Learning of the Schools*. Ithaca: Cornell University Press.

Garber, D. 1986. "*Semel in vita*: The Scientific Background to Descartes's *Meditations*." In: A. Rorty, ed., *Essays on Descartes's Meditations*. Berkeley and Los Angeles: University of California Press, pp. 81-116.

Garber, D. 1988. "Descartes, the Aristotelians, and the Revolution that did not happen in 1637." *The Monist*. 77: 471-486.

Garber, D. 1991. *Descartes's Metaphysical Physics*. Chicago: University of Chicago Press.

Gaukroger, S., ed. 1980. *Descartes: Philosophy, Mathematics and Physics*. Brighton: Harvester.

Gilson, E. 1913a. *Index scholastico-cartésien*. Paris: Alcan.

Gilson, E. 1913b. *La Liberté chez Descartes et la Théologie*. Paris: Alcan.

Gilson, E., ed., 1926 (4th ed., 1967). *Descartes. Discours de la Méthode. Textes et Commentaires*. Paris: Vrin.

Gilson, E. 1930 (4th ed., 1965). *Etudes sur le Rôle de la Pensée Médiévale dans la Formation du Système Cartésien*. Paris: Vrin.

Gilson, E. 1947. *History of Philosophy and Philosophical Education*. Milwaukee: Marquette University Press.

Gilson, E. 1951. *Wisdom and Love in St. Thomas*. Milwaukee: Marquette University Press.

Gouhier, H. 1978. *Cartésianisme et Augustinisme au XVIIe Siècle*. Paris: Vrin.

Grene, M. 1985. *Descartes*. Minneapolis: University of Minnesota Press.

Grene, M. 1986. "Die Einheit des Menschen: Descartes unter den Scholastikern." *Dialectica*. 40: 209-222.

Hatfield, G. 1985. "First Philosophy and Natural Philosophy in Descartes." In: A. J. Holland, ed., *Philosophy, Its History and Historiography*. Dordrecht: Reidel, pp. 149-164.

Hatfield, G. 1986. "The Senses and the Fleshless Eye: The Meditations as Cognitive Exercises." In: Rorty, A., ed., *Essays on Descartes's Meditations*. Berkeley and Los Angeles: University of California Press, pp. 45-80.

Hatfield, G. 1988. "Science, Certainty and Descartes." *PSA* 1988. 2: 249-262.

Hoffman, P. 1986. "The Unity of Descartes's Man." *Phil. Rev.* 90: 339-370.

Marion, J.-L. 1981. *Sur la Théologie Blanche de Descartes*. Paris: Presses Universitaires de France.

Rodis-Lewis, G. 1986. "On the Complementarity of Meditations III and V: From the 'General Rule' of Evidence to 'Certain Science.'" In: Rorty, A., ed., *Essays on Descartes's Meditations*. Berkeley and Los Angeles: University of California Press, pp. 271-296.

Rorty, A., ed. 1986. *Essays on Descartes's Meditations*. Berkeley and Los Angeles: University of California Press.

Schuster, J. A. 1980. "Descartes' *Mathesis Universalis*, 1619-1628." In: Gaukroger, S., ed., *Descartes: Philosophy, Mathematics and Physics*. Brighton: Harvester, pp. 41-96.

Weber, J.-P. 1964. *La Constitution du Texte des Regulae*. Paris: Societé d'Edition d'Enseignement Supérieur.

Wells, N. J. 1967. "Objective being: Descartes and his Sources." *The Modern Schoolman*. 45: 49-61.

Wells, N. J. 1990. "Objective reality of Ideas in Descartes, Caterus and Suarez." *J. Hist. Phil.* 28: 33-61.

Wolfson, H. A. 1934. *The Philosophy of Spinoza*. 2 vols. Cambridge, MA: Harvard University Press.

The Aquinas Lectures
Published by the Marquette University Press
Milwaukee, Wisconsin 53233
United States of America
= =

#1   **St. Thomas and the Life of Learning.** John F. McCormick, S.J. (1937).

ISBN 0-87462-101-1

#2   **St. Thomas and the Gentiles.** Mortimer J. Adler (1938).

ISBN 0-87462-102-X

#3   **St. Thomas and the Greeks.** Anton C. Pegis (1939).

ISBN 0-87462-103-8

#4   **The Nature and Functions of Authority.** Yves Simon (1940).

ISBN 0-87462-104-6

#5   **St. Thomas and Analogy.** Gerald B. Phelan (1941).

ISBN 0-87462-105-4

#6   **St. Thomas and the Problem of Evil.** Jacques Maritain (1942).

ISBN 0-87462-106-2

#7   **Humanism and Theology.** Werner Jaeger (1943).

ISBN 0-87462-107-0

#8   **The Nature and Origins of Scientism.** John Wellmuth (1944).

ISBN 0-87462-108-9

#9   **Cicero in the Courtroom of St. Thomas Aquinas.** E. K. Rand (1945).

ISBN 0-87462-109-7

#10   **St. Thomas and Epistemology.** Louis Marie Regis, O.P. (1946).

ISBN 0-87462-110-0

#11   **St. Thomas and the Greek Moralists.** Vernon J. Bourke (1947).

ISBN 0-87462-111-9

#12   **History of Philosophy and Philosophical Education.** Etienne Gilson (1947).

ISBN 0-87462-112-7

#13   **The Natural Desire for God.** William R. O'Connor (1948).
ISBN 0-87462-113-5

#14   **St. Thomas and the World State.** Robert M. Hutchins (1949).
ISBN O-87462-114-3

#15   **Method in Metaphysics.** Robert J. Henle, S.J. (1950).
ISBN 0-87462-115-1

#16   **Wisdom and Love in St. Thomas Aquinas.** Etienne Gilson (1951).

ISBN 0-87462-116-X

#17   **The Good in Existential Metaphysics.** Elizabeth G. Salmon (1952).

ISBN 0-87462-117-8

#18   **St. Thomas and the Object of Geometry.** Vincent Edward Smith (1953).

ISBN 0-87462-118-6

#19   **Realism and Nominalism Revisited.** Henry Veatch (1954).
ISBN 0-87462-119-4

#20   **Imprudence in St. Thomas Aquinas.** Charles J. O'Neil (1955).
ISBN 0-87462-120-8

#21   **The Truth that Frees.** Gerard Smith, S.J. (1956).
ISBN 0-87462-121-6

#22   **St. Thomas and the Future of Metaphysics.** Joseph Owens (1957).

ISBN 0-87462-122-4

#23   **Thomas and the Physics of 1958 A Confrontation.** Henry Margenau (1958).

ISBN 0-87462-123-2

#24   **Metaphysics and Ideology.** William O. Martin (1959).
ISBN 0-8746S-124-0

#25   **Language, Truth, and Poetry.** Victor M. Hamm (1960).
ISBN 0-87462-125-9

#26   **Metaphysics and Historicity.** Emil L. Fackenheim (1961).
ISBN 0-87462-126-7

#27   **The Lure of Wisdom.** James D. Collins (1962).
ISBN 0-87462-127-5

#28   **Religion and Art.** Paul Weiss (1963).

ISBN 0-87462-128-3

#29   **St. Thomas and Philosophy.** Anton C. Pegis (1964).
ISBN 0-87462-129-1

#30   **The University in Process.** John O. Riedl (1965).
ISBN 0-87462-130-5

#31   **The Pragmatic Meaning of God.** Robert O. Johann (1966).
ISBN O-87462-131-3

#32   **Religion and Empiricism.** John E. Smith (1967).
ISBN 0-87462-132-1

#33   **The Subject.** Bernard Lonergan, S.J. (1968).
ISBN 0-87462-133-X

#34   **Beyond Trinity.** Bernard J. Cooke (1969).
ISBN 0-87462-134-8

#35   **Ideas and Concepts.** Julius R. Weinberg (1970).
ISBN 0-87462-135-6

#36   **Reason and Faith Revisited.** Francis H. Parker (1971).
ISBN 0-87462-136-4

#37   **Psyche and Cerebrum.** John N. Findlay (1972).
ISBN 0-87462-137-2

#38   **The Problem of the Criterion.** Roderick M. Chisholm (1973).
ISBN 0-87462-138-0

#39   **Man as Infinite Spirit.** James H. Robb (1974).
ISBN 0-87462-139-9

#40 **Aquinas to Whitehead: Seven Centuries of Metaphysics of Religion.** Charles E. Hartshorne (1976).

ISBN 0-87462-141-0

#41 **The Problem of Evil.** Errol E. Harris (1977).

ISBN 0-87462-142-9

#42 **The Catholic University and the Faith.** Francis C. Wade, S.J. (1978).

ISBN 0-87462-143-7

#43 **St. Thomas and Historicity.** Armand Maurer, C.S.B. (1979).

ISBN 0-87462-144-5

#44 **Does God Have a Nature?** Alvin Plantinga (1980).

ISBN 0-87462-145-3

#45 **Rhyme and Reason: St. Thomas and Modes of Discourse.** Ralph McInerny (1981).

ISBN 0-87462-148-8

#46 **The Gift: Creation.** Kenneth L. Schmitz (1982).

ISBN 0-87462-149-6

#47 **How Philosophy Begins.** Beatrice H. Zedler (1983).

ISBN 0-87462-151-8

#48 **The Reality of the Historical Past.** Paul Ricoeur (1984).

ISBN 0-87462-152-6

#49 **Human Ends and Human Actions.** Alan Donagan (1985).

ISBN 0-87462-153-4

#50   **Imagination and Metaphysics in St. Augustine.** Robert J. O'Connell, S.J. (1986).

ISBN 0-87462-227-1

#51   **Expectations of Immortality in Late Antiquity.** A. Hilary Armstrong (1987).

ISBN 0-87462-154-2

#52.   **The Self.** Anthony Kenny (1988).

ISBN 0-87462-155-0

#53.   **The Nature of Philosophical Inquiry.** Quentin P. Lauer, S.J. (1989).

ISBN 0-87462-156-9

#54.   **First Principles, Final Ends and Contemporary Philosophical Issues.** Alasdair MacIntyre (1990).

ISBN 0-87462-157-7

#55.   **Descartes Among the Scholastics.** Marjorie Grene (1991).
ISBN 0-87462-158-5

Uniform format, cover, and binding.

Copies of this Aquinas Lecture and the others in the series are obtainable from:

Marquette University Press
Marquette University
Milwaukee, Wisconsin 53233, U.S.A.

Publishers of: *Medieval Philosophical Texts in Translation
                      *Pere Marquette Theology Lectures
                      *St. Thomas Aquinas Lectures
                      *Philosophy & Theology (journal)